Winter Scenes
COLORING BOOK

MARTY NOBLE

DOVER PUBLICATIONS, INC.
MINEOLA, NEW YORK

The winter season brings joy and ethereal beauty to the world. This gallery of winter scenes depicts pristine snow-covered villages, panoramic landscapes, and exuberant children bundled up in scarves and gloves to play in the snow. This collection also includes images of fun winter sports such as skiing, ice skating on frozen ponds, and riding in a horse-drawn sled. Specially designed for the experienced colorist, the illustrations in this book will keep you warm and cozy while you experiment with color and different media. Each of the thirty-one plates has been perforated for removal to make displaying your work easy.

Bibliographical Note
Winter Scenes Coloring Book is a new work, first published by Dover Publications, Inc., in 2014.

International Standard Book Number
ISBN-13: 978-0-486-79190-6
ISBN-10: 0-486-79190-4

Manufactured in the United States by RR Donnelley
79190411   2015
www.doverpublications.com

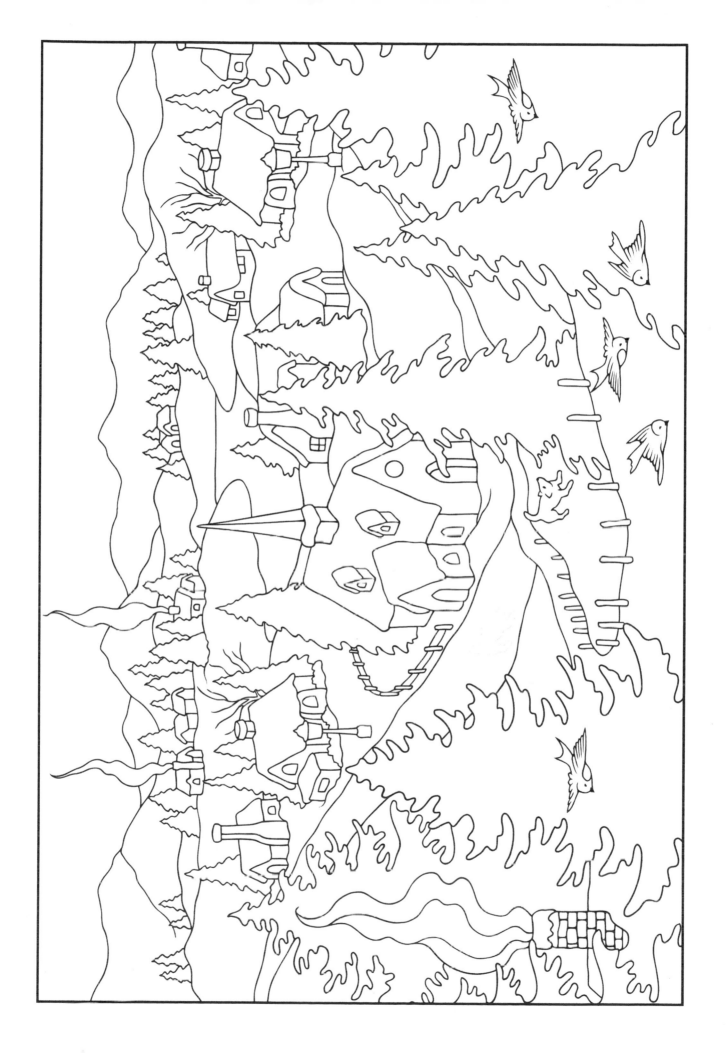